Winning in Life!

Helping your children to put God first when dealing with life's challenges

ALISON WOMACK

WOMACK HOUSE PUBLISHING

©2021 by Alison Womack

WINNING IN LIFE!

All rights reserved. In accordance with the U.S. copyright Act of 1976, the scanning, uploading, and electronic sharing of any part of this book without permission of the publisher constitute unlawful piracy and theft of the author's intellectual property. If you would like to use material from the book (other than for review purposes), prior written permission must be obtained by contacting the publisher at permissions at www.womackhouse.com

This publication is designed to provide experienced based authoritative information in regard to the subject matter covered. The publisher is not engaged in rendering psychological, financial, or legal service. It is sold with the understanding that if professional counseling assistance is needed in any area, it should be sought.

Scripture quotations taken from the King James Version.
Copyright 1954,1958,1962,1964,1965,1987 by The Lockman Foundation. Used by permission.
Scripture quotations are from the ESV Bible (The Holy Bible, English Standard Version), copyright 2001 By Crossway, a publishing ministry of Good News Publishers. Used by permission. All rights reserved.

Womack House Publishing, LLC.
3965 East Brookstown Drive
Baton Rouge, LA. 70805
www.womackhouse.com
Publishing Consultant: Tonia Askins of Cultivate Press
Printed in the United States of America
ISBN: 978-1-7375713-0-8 (pbk)
Library of Congress Cataloging -in- Publication Data applied for
The publisher is not responsible for websites (or other content) that are not owned by the publisher.
The Womack House name and logo are trademarks of Womack House Publishing, LLC.
For information about special discounts for bulk purchases, speaking engagements or interviews contact Womack House Publishing via email at info@womackhouse.com or call 1-844-598-6654.

TABLE OF CONTENTS

Introduction 1
Chapter 1- Self Esteem 6
Chapter 2 - Protection.. 13
Chapter 3 - Behavior 17
Chapter 4 – Making Good Decisions.......................... 25
Chapter 5 – Confidence.. 30
Chapter 6 - Trouble Learning...................................... 35
Chapter 7 – Health Challenges 41
Chapter 8 – Children Adjusting To Divorce................. 47
Chapter 9 – Children Adjusting To A Blended Family . 53
Chapter 10 - God's Favor For Your Life 57

INTRODUCTION

Our children are gifts from God. We, as parents, are our children's role models. What have you said or put in your children's lives today that will help them tomorrow--physically, spiritually, mentally, and emotionally?

What type of environment are you setting for your children? Is it an environment of positive words or negative words? It doesn't matter how you were raised and who spoke over your life, you can change your child's destiny by saying positive affirmations or positive words to your child or children and molding it into their spirit. It doesn't matter how you feel or what you see environmentally. Let go of your emotions!

God loves us so much that He gave us a road map to follow to live the best life and to thrive. Will it be easy? No, but with God, all things are possible. We want our children to be strong, confident, and loved.

This is how you do it-- with positive words and professing God's word day and night until it stays in their hearts. You profess until you get the results you desire.

So, what are your children dealing with today? Not feeling love & accepted? Fear of the unknown? Low self-esteem? Behavior problems? God wants us to take His word and profess it over our children to cover and protect them with a firewall of protection, no matter where they are or what they are doing. You have to put God's word in your children to give them a good foundation. That foundation is strength, confidence, love, and power to overcome challenges they will face from the age of three into adulthood.

We want our children to learn how to make good decisions, not based on their environment and what they see, but based on God's word. When we teach our children to profess God's word, it builds up a child's belief system. **<u>Belief System</u>** *is a set of* *principles or tenets which together form the basis of a religion, philosophy, or moral code.*

<u>From the Bible dictionary</u>, *it says, faith is a belief in or confident attitude toward God, involving commitment to his will for one's life.*

The more you say something and the more you hear it, the more your inner ear picks it up and it gets into your heart. You start to believe it, feel it, and then see it.

<u>Example</u>: *If you say, "I have a big nose or I am tired" and you say that every day, you start to believe it. Then you start to see the nose getting bigger and you begin feeling that way. Then your body carries it out.*

We are to say what God says... I have a beautiful nose and I am strong and full of energy. **<u>Psalm 139:14</u> says I am fearfully and wonderfully made and Philippians 4:13 says,** *I can do all things through Christ who strengthens me. God* *loves us so much that he gave parents instructions. The same way that our children must obey us, we must obey God's commandments. The bible says in* **_Proverbs 18:21_**, *"Death and Life are in the power of the tongue: and they that love it shall eat the fruit thereof." We are speaking spirits, so we have the power to choose blessing over cursing, life over death. We must profess over our children daily and say what God says about them.*

Here are professions that God laid on my heart to put together for my children. I am going to tell you why we should speak nothing but faith filled words over our children's life. We must give our children a strong foundation through God's word to let them know they cannot be stopped no matter what the circumstances because God is their source.

We must speak God's word like watering a seed to produce a plant. It takes time, patience, prayer and consistency for the plant to grow.

WHO ARE YOU GOING TO LET DETERMINE YOUR CHILDREN'S FUTURE? WHO ARE YOU GOING TO LET RAISE YOUR CHILDREN? SOCIETY, TEACHERS, OR GOD'S WORD?

Chapter 1- Self Esteem

All children come from different environments and some may feel a lack of acceptance at school, based on how they are being treated or insecurities they may have for various reasons. For example, some parents compare siblings and it may cause some children to feel they need to compete or change themselves to receive love and acceptance. All children are unique in their own way and should not be compared. Do you compare your children?

Some children can let things go through one ear and out the other. They have the ability to let it go, but they still feel some type of way about it, whether happy or sad. Those are the emotions the child must channel in a positive way and not in a negative way:

According to Self-Esteem and Being You by Anita Naik, *self-esteem is having a good or just opinion of oneself and that means trusting and believing in yourself.*

*Why is **self-esteem** crucial?*

***1**. People (also children) achieve more when they believe in themselves.*

***2**. Self-Esteem means having the confidence to be yourself.*

***3**. If you have self-esteem, you'll respect yourself and when you respect yourself everyone who knows you will as well.*

***4**. You will know that it is more important to live up to your own expectations than to struggle to fulfill what others are expecting of you (i.e., friends).*

***5**. Self-Esteem means that you don't have to prove anything to anyone.*

***6**. You'll be much happier knowing that you're being honest with yourself and others.*

Measuring ourselves against these outside standards is fine when everything is going well, but, when it's not, don't let unhelpful comments make you feel worthless, depressed, and insecure.

You don't need unhealthy thoughts. You must say what God says.

We must tell our children that Jesus loves all the children in the world, it doesn't matter what race you are whether you are yellow, red, black, brown or white. Jesus loves all the children of the world the same.

In society, you will meet different parents with various opinions regarding equality in race and speak and act negatively. We must be very careful with our words and teach our children equality and fairness.

<u>Example</u>: *If Johnny was teased by friends about having a big head, not being able to read, or looking different because of the color of his skin, it will affect his self-esteem.*

Susan is skinny. She is teased at school and at home. This will cause her to begin comparing herself to every girl around her and it will affect her self-esteem.

Bella always gets praise because she does well at school and stays on green for her behavior. Brian doesn't always stay on green, so he doesn't get candy or gifts at all. Then Bella and Brian's mom, Mary, always compares them and say if you be more like Bella, you would get candy. You just don't listen.

Parents, we must not compare our children because every child copes differently and can feel unloved. Your child will grow up comparing themselves to their siblings, friends, or family members. That's when jealousy, resentment, and other things come to the mind. You have opened up the door for Satan to walk right into it and add to what's being said in the mind.

Many children may laugh off the negative words and some might hold it in and cry at night or start to lash out at people. Both are *negative emotions and will cause it to affect their self-esteem. Those are negative emotions and wounds from not being treated correctly. After situations of rejection, we must tell and show our children that God loves all of us so much that He died for us (**John 3:16**). We are the righteousness of God in Christ. We are covered by God's love and He made us and loves us just the way we are. We must tell our children they are speaking spirits and they have the power to say what God says. I am loved, I am beautiful, I am handsome, I am accepted, and I am loved by God just the way I am. We must talk to our children and make sure that they do not feel a lack of acceptance. We do not want it to transform their personalities into something unhealthy, like anger or depression. Let them know God made everyone different in the image and likeness of Him.*

Here is an exercise I do with my children. It is a high and low exercise we do every day to communicate when they come from school. We take a few minutes and talk about their day, how it was, what was the high that made them feel their happiest at school, and what the low was for the day that made them feel sad at school. Then, we talk about how we can make it better because tomorrow is a new day for a new beginning.

<u>Children's Prayer:</u> *Father in the name of Jesus, I thank you for loving me so much and for dying on the cross for me. I am strong in God and confident because I am beautiful / handsome and precious in your sight no matter what anyone says. You love me just the way I am. I am walking in your image and likeness. I trust it and believe only what God's word says about me. I do not receive any negative words or negative thoughts about me from teachers, friends, or family. I will not allow it in my mind or heart because I know you love me.*

So, I call for positive words and positive energy around me now, in Jesus' Name. Amen

<u>Parents' Prayer</u>: *Father God, in the Name of Jesus. I bind and cast down any negative words that anyone have told my child or spoken over him/her that has made him/her feel rejected, unloved, ugly, or sad. I cast out anything that is not from you. I loose positive feelings of love, joy, and peace. My child has happy thoughts and a normal emotional state. He/She is wanted, accepted and loved because Jesus died on the cross for them and I thank you that your love is real and surrounding him/her and filling them up each day. Show me how to teach them to channel their emotions in a way that pleases you. Amen*

It is a mean world out there and we must prepare our children for it. Let them know that their self-worth is not determined by people, but by God.

Chapter 2- Protection

In our society today, we must teach our children that Jesus is our best friend, and He is always there for us. We must tell our children God is big, strong, and mighty and He cares for them and sends angels across the earth. I would tell my children to talk to God and tell him how you feel. Also, that God does not give us the Spirit of fear. He gives us power, love, and a sound mind. **2 Timothy 1:7 says,** *"He also wants us to be strong and courageous! Do not be afraid or discouraged God is with you wherever you go." (Reference:* **Joshua 1:9b***)*

Example*: One day, I was driving in my truck with my children and it started to rain lightly. Five minutes later, it began thundering and lightning, raining very heavily and fast-- to the point that you could barely see the road. So, I pulled over for a few minutes and my son said, "Oh, no what are we going to do"? My daughter said she was* *scared. I told them to sit back and stay calm! Don't be afraid because you can't think when you are scared, you panic and you will not make the right decision in panic mode. I told them God loves us and He promised to protect us. So, we must call for our angels to protect us. I told my Children God has angels everywhere, so let's be a speaking spirit. Let's call for peace in the* **atmosphere** *and say peace be still, rain calm down and thunder stop now, in Jesus Name. We took a deep breath and started singing, my God is so great, so strong, and so mighty, its nothing my God cannot do! Then we said together, God does not give me a spirit of fear. He gives me power, love, and a sound mind. I told them sometime when you pray or call for your angels, the devil heightens the situation and makes you feel like God or the angels didn't hear you. Like when the rain came down harder after we prayed and spoke to it. We must trust God's word and believe it even when we do not see it or feel like it. Shortly after I* *got back on the road and the weather calmed down, I was able to drive us home, safe and sound.*

Childrens' Prayer: *Father God, in the name of Jesus, you said you are my best friend and always there for me. You said to be strong and brave because you love me, and you promised to protect me and care for me. So, you didn't give me the spirit of fear, you gave me power, love, and a sound mind, in Jesus' name. I choose to not fear but have faith in you. Amen*

Parents' Prayer: *I thank you God for my children's safety. Shield them with a firewall of protection. Let them know by your spirit that they are not alone and cover their bodies physically, spiritually, mentally, and emotionally. Keep them from all hurt, harm, and danger of any kind from the devil. Thank you, God, for giving them peace and strength that surpasses all understanding everywhere they go.*

No weapon formed against them shall prosper, in Jesus' name, Amen.

Chapter 3- Behavior

In society today, children feel unloved and unwanted by the words that come out of people's mouth. In large part, due to different or difficult environments. Children have feelings, stresses, and worries about things just like adults. We must consider their feelings! It does not matter what age they are. Children's minds are like a sponge and it starts at birth. Also, how the child is talked to or treated commonly leads to their behavior and if you (as a parent) talk down to your child, the child will be defiant. We, as parents, play a major role in our children's behavior. Every child needs tender love and care, no matter how they look, feel, or carry themselves. Each child needs structure and a regular routine.

According to **THE 5 LOVE LANGUAGES OF CHILDREN** *by* **Dr. Gary Chapman & Ross Campbell, M.D.***, the parent's responsibility is to keep their children* *emotional love tanks full, using all the love languages while focusing on his/her primary language. Nothing makes a child more desperate than a lack of love. It does not make sense to demand good behavior from a child without first making sure he/she is feeling loved. Gary Chapman lists the love languages as:*

***1**- Physical Touch*

***2**- Quality Time*

***3**- Gifts*

***4**- Words of Affirmation*

***5**- Acts of Service*

We must observe our children to see what they ask of us the most to determine what they need.

I feel like with God all things are possible, no matter how hard it gets. **Proverbs 3:6** *says, "In all thy ways acknowledge God and he will direct thy paths." We must stay* *in faith and not go by our emotions and use God's word in our life, daily, including with our children. Will it be challenging, yes, but we know with God on our side and staying focused, it can be done. Children will test you, so when your child is acting bad or being disrespectful, continue to reassure your love to them and correct them.*

<u>Example</u>: *I went into the store one day and gave my children clear instructions that I am not going to buy any candy today. My children just had Raising Cane's for lunch and were not hungry or tired. As we begin to checkout, my children asked for candy. I bent down, and looked them in the face, and told them we discussed this already, let me pay for my groceries.*

One of my children started crying and then he got louder and louder. I walked out of the store with my groceries and put my children in the car.

Here are the steps I used:

Step 1- *Prayer. God, I am acknowledging you right now. I have given my children instruction and one is not being obedient (by hollering for candy). Show me how to show him love in a way that is pleasing to you.*

Step 2- *My son love language is physical touch and words of affirmation. His primary language is physical touch. So, I went over to him to tell him to calm down and gave him a hug affirming that it is OK.*

Step 3– *Next, I selected an appropriate way to train him through punishment. What was more effective to him was taking something away that he enjoyed for a few hours to let him know he can't act the way he did in the store. He must express himself through words, not hollering or yelling.*

Step 4- *I will reassure him for the rest of the day and weeks to make sure he feels loved by targeting his primary love* *languages with hugs and kisses and words of affirmation…saying you can do it; you are a good listener.*

Step 5– *Now, he says his affirmations each morning by reciting, "I am a good listener, I am discipline, I obey my parents and teachers, I will follow direction the first time, and even when it's hard, I will stick with it and refuse to quit. I will take a deep breath count to 10 and I think things through."*

Sometimes when children feel unloved or need attention they lash out and begin to have behavior problems. We may not like the behavior. However, if the child feels desperate enough they will demand attention, through inappropriate behavior. Nothing makes a child more desperate than a lack of love. However, it does not make sense to demand good behavior from a child without first making sure he/she feels love.

Here are some steps that has helped me along the way:

***1**. Acknowledging God- pray over your children every day to cover them.*

***2**. Find out your child's primary Love Language and focus on that, making sure they feel loved. No matter how your child is physically.*

***3**. Select an appropriate way to train your child through punishment.*

***4**. I make sure I speak my children's Love Language daily to make sure their Love Tank stays full.*

A child that misbehaves may have needs that need to be addressed that is being overlooked. Providing attention in a lacked area may prevent misbehavior.

Ask yourself, "What can I do to correct my child's behavior?"

We, as parents, have a responsibility regarding protecting our children's emotional health. We must keep our children emotional love tanks full by speaking their primary language.

When a child misbehaves, automatically, some parents think punishment. But as parents, we need to select an appropriate way to train a child according to scripture.

Parents' prayer: *Father God, in the name of Jesus, in all my ways, I acknowledge you and submit to you by my spirit. Show me how to keep my children's emotional love tanks full, so they won't act out in anger by hollering, kicking or screaming. I want them using their words to express themselves in a positive way and in a way that pleases you. Show me how to correct my child's behavior with your love. Help me to discern when to use their love language effectively in their lives, so they can be fulfilled emotionally.*

Father God, cover my children with your love to let them know they are needed and wanted. I bind up confusion in their minds and bodies and the thing that will stop them from being obedient. Amen

<u>Childrens' prayer:</u> *Father God, thank you for loving me and listening to me even when I don't obey my parents or teachers. Please forgive me when I am being disobedient or angry. Show me how-to walk with love and express my feeling in words when I don't feel loved. Let me speak in a way that pleases you.*

I am disciplined! I am loved! The peace of God is in me! In the name of Jesus, Amen.

Chapter 4 – Making Good Decisions

In society today, our children are being influenced by many things. They care about what's on TV, social media, what songs are popular, and what their peers think in school. Their environment at home is important. Children learn by what they see and hear. If they see stealing, bullying, selfishness, peer pressure and hatred that's what is being put in their hearts.

Example: *I told John to go to school and during lunch, not to play with his milk so he won't waste it or I may tell him, "Don't play at the lunch table with your food because you have other people sitting on side of you. Be good and obey." John went to school and during lunch time, John started playing with his milk and food because Daniel and the other children were playing with their milk and food. In consequence, John was the only one out of the whole class who wasted his milk everywhere on his clothes* and on the table. So, the teacher took 5 minutes off everyone's recess time and John had to stay back and clean up his mess. He had two extra minutes taken away from his recess by not making a good choice to obey and not be influenced by others.

Will it be easy for the Children? NO, but they must learn that every decision they make has consequences, whether it's good or bad.

Example: Being around children that curse and do not obey their teachers is a bad choice.

Bad choice – John didn't listen and loses some recess time.

So parents, our job, according to the Bible is to (**Proverbs 22:6**) train up a child in the way he/she should go, even when they are old, they will not depart from it.

If you keep your children around an environment of people (smoking, drinking, cursing, lying, and cheating), no matter how good they are, they will become influenced to do the things they have seen by their environment.

God gives us rules to stay safe.

How is that DONE? By what you affirm or say over your child every day.

According to **Train up a Child by Chuck Sturgeon,** *children become what they learn from experiences in the home. Their characters are formed by mom and dad. A child's personality, strengths, weaknesses, attitudes, and values are formed in a large part by his/her parents.*

Good choice *– John goes home, and his mom tells him to clean his room because she will check his room in 20 minutes. John put his iPad down and cleaned his room in 10 minutes then he told his mom he was done. She checked his room, and he* *received a treat and was able to start back playing on his iPad. If he did not, the iPad would have been taken from him for the rest of the day. There is a consequence for not listening.*

Also, according to **Train Up a Child by Chuck Sturgeon**, you must be an example. Take time with your children. When you want them to do something that is new to them, show them exactly how to perform the task. Don't have an older brother or sister show them. Let each child know he/she is equally important to you and worth your time. Remember, one of the definitions of train is to instruct by exercise.

We must teach our children to obey authority because there are consequences when they don't obey. Life will teach them lessons that are not good in a way that is not pleasing to God if we don't first guide them in the correct way.

So, if they want to make God happy and subsequently you as a parent happy, they must obey even when its hard and stick with it and refuse to quit.

Have the attitude of love with your child all the time. Don't be the one to always point out your child's faults. Tell them you have faith in them to do better in their weaker points.

Remember your words have <u>POWER</u>!

Chapter 5 – Confidence

Confidence is key and one of the ways I have helped my children build their confidence is with mirror exercises. Children should look in the mirror and say I am strong, I am beautiful, I am handsome, I am loved, and I am the righteousness of God in Christ Jesus. No matter how I feel, He is there. I also tell my children if they want to grow up to be strong and wise and live long on the earth, they must obey. "No one can stop you and determine your future but you."

I also explain that when they make bad choices, they must apologize to us, their parents or teachers and then repent to God next. "We, your parents love you so much, but God loves you more."

*According to **A Power of Self- Confidence by Brian Tracy,** the Law of Concentration says, "Anything you dwell upon grows in your reality." Anything that you think about* *long enough or hard enough, eventually becomes a part of your mental process, exerting its influence and power on your attitude and your behavior.*

In this sense, you are a self-made man or woman. You are where you are and what you are because of the thoughts you have allowed to preoccupy your mind and eventually became a part of your character and your personality.

In that regard, you must constantly think on thoughts of boldness and being courageous, unshakable, and with determination going into the **No Fear Zone**. *You must know that when facing big and small challenges in your life, you must be completely unafraid, convinced of your ability to accomplish anything you put your mind to.*

I tell my Children, "You are smart strong and able, so when you have big or small challenges no problem is too big for you when you acknowledge God. He wants to help you. God will show you solutions to the problem."

Example: *If your children fall off their bike, make a low grade on a test, learn new work, get a wrong answer in class, or teased for how they dress or act, you are to encourage them. You would first explain to them what God says, I am the righteousness of God in Christ Jesus. I am strong and mighty because Jesus lives in me. I will not be stopped; I can't be stopped, Tell them, take a deep breath and try again because tomorrow is a new day and a new beginning. Your confidence is in God, not in people. God's grace and love renews us each day. I tell my children we have a big God, and we can do big things with him.*

Childrens' Affirmation:

Step 1- *I take a deep breath and count to 10 when I am under pressure or feeling sad or not capable.*

Step 2- *I say, Father God in the Name of Jesus give me the ability, strength and courage to trust and know you are always near to watch over me.*

Step 3- *I am strong, I am an overcomer each and every day. I make good decisions because my trust is in you, Lord. I follow directions and I listen. I stick with things and refuse to quit because **Philippians 4:13** says, "I can do all things through Christ who strengthens me."*

Every situation God brings me out, my confidence gets stronger in Him, each and every day.

Parents' Prayer:

God, your word says train up a child in the way he should go, even when he is old, he/she will not depart from it. Show me how to teach my children how to have confidence in you to let them know you are always nearby. Help me to teach my children how to make good decisions and to please you, so they can live long on the earth and when they don't, to quickly repent. Teach me how to be patient and consistent in showing them in times when they are feeling weak, tempted, scared or afraid, that you are their strength. Teach me how to encourage my children how to say no to peer pressure, bullying, selfishness, and most of all, breaking rules. God, you have given rules and directions to keep everyone safe. Let me direct them and teach them that its consequences to every decision they make. In the name of Jesus, Amen.

Chapter 6 - Trouble Learning

Does your child have trouble learning things or comprehending things? It is ok, it will be alright. God loves you and your child, and He will give you directions on what to do if you acknowledge Him. When you find out things about your child that need to be improved, thank God for the information because now, you know how to cater to your child's needs and what it will take to make him/her better. I have learned through the years, with God, all things are possible.

YOUR WORDS ARE THE MOST POWERFUL THING ON THE FACE OF THE EARTH. *We are our children's speaking spirits until our children get to the age of accountability where they understand the importance of words and that they can speak positive or negative over their life. We are responsible as parents to speak into their lives. The words we say today creates your* *tomorrow. I know it can be scary or overwhelming, but God is our helper and source with big challenges and little challenges. You will discover with God's help; you can do very big things!*

According to Help Guide's Tips for Dealing with your Child's Learning Disability:

1. Keep things in perspective. A learning disability is not insurmountable....

2. Become your own expert....

3. Be an advocate for your child.

4. Remember that your influence outweighs all others.

5. Clarify your goals.

6. Be a good listener.

7. Offer new solutions.

8. Keep the focus.

We, as parents, must acknowledge God in every area, especially with our children. I declare God's word over my children day and night. We must teach them how to profess God's word over their lives to prepare them for adulthood.

<u>Example</u>: *At the age of three, my son got tested at a learning center. It was recommended that he needs to take some speech therapy classes so he can work on his social skills. I made a plan that I would read to him every night and make sure he learns everything for his age level, but that was not enough. Did I want to hear that? No, but God put someone in my life to help me with the things I didn't know, things that would prepare him for his future. Now, I know what to spiritually pray for. That showed me that I had to get up, put my feeling to the side and take action. Faith without works is dead, so I put my son in a learning center that works on his social* *skills, but also gives him more structure and assistance with his behavior.*

The devil will automatically put in your head the negative thoughts that something is wrong with your child. I heard what the lady told me, but I didn't receive it in my mind. I said my child is smart, he has good structure, and focus. God wants to help us in ways we can't imagine, so he sent me help because I asked for it. I just had to go through the process, maintain positive thoughts and remember God's word. My son had two semesters of speech therapy and it gave him direction, focus, and structure. The help I received educated me as a mom and gave me direction as well, especially with how to be better at caring for his specific needs. It helped a lot, and my son is doing great! To God be the Glory!

We can't always look at issues that may arise in a negative way. We have to look at the good in everything, no matter what. In addition, put yourself around like-minded people.

PLEASE DO NOT TREAT YOUR CHILD AS WHAT THE DOCTOR, SPECIALIST OR TEACHER SAID, BUT TREAT AND SEE YOUR CHLD AS THE END RESULT. THE END RESULT IS WHAT GOD'S WORD SAYS ABOUT THE SITUATION. MAJORITY OF THE TIME, WE AS PARENTS WILL BECOME FEARFUL, SCARED OR DEFENSIVE ABOUT THEIR CHILD. YOU MUST LIVE IN FAITH NOT FEAR AND BELIEVE GOD IS IN CONTROL AND WILL SEE YOU THROUGH.

<u>Childrens' Prayer</u>: *I can do all things through Christ who strengthens me. I have the mind of Christ. No weapon formed against me shall prosper. I am smart. I can learn. I am 10 times better than the world. I am disciplined and focused. I comprehend everything set before me, even when it's hard. I can take a deep breath, think things through, and I refuse to quit because God is my helper and strength. Now, show me the way because God, I know you are always there for me, In Jesus' name, Amen.*

Parents' Prayer: *Father, I know that with you all things are possible. Show me how to be a good parent who teaches my Children to be focused, disciplined, and to have good structure in life. Show me how to teach them to stand strong when negative words or negative situations are spoken over them. Show me how to think the best in every situation, trusting and knowing that with help, you will bring us out on top and rising in every lesson. Anything that is negative, I know, is not from you because every good and perfect gift comes from you, God. Amen*

Chapter 7 – Health Challenges

Many children grow up today with different health challenges, but we must teach them to have a positive attitude. No matter what they are going through, God loves them and knows about their health problems. We must tell our children that our God is mighty and powerful and there is nothing our God can't do. He still heal, deliver, and set free children, when they believe. Jesus died for every sickness, every disease and anything that will stop them from living a productive life. Will it be easy? No, but God has blessed us in this world with doctors and physicians. Yet still, he doesn't want us to put nothing before Him.

God is our source, and he gives doctors wisdom, knowledge and understanding in how to treat people. We, as parents, must always acknowledge God, so his angels can go before you to give direction. Then go to the doctor and when we go, we will get clarity and direction on the problem or situation at hand. Here are my steps in overcoming health problems with your child(ren):

Step 1: *Pray & acknowledge God for direction and to give your angels charge or access to work for you.*

Step 2: *Go to the doctor, (but you must be prepared for any negative words you hear stay calm, listen, but don't receive in your mind).*

Step 3: *Pray over the medicine to cover your child's body, read directions and side effects of them, then let them take the medicine.*

We must teach and show our children how to have faith in God and trust His word even when we don't feel or see anything or when we don't hear from God.

Example: *When my son was younger, late one Saturday night, he had a very high* *fever. It was out of the blue and it shook me a bit because the day before he was feeling great and he went to sleep like normal. He woke up very hot, sweaty, and shaking. I said, "Oh my goodness what is going on." I immediately prayed and acknowledged God that he is healed by the stripes of Jesus and he will live and not die. I declared the word of the Lord. He still had a fever, but I gave my angels something to do to cover my son until we could find out the problem.*

It was very late, so I called his pediatrician, and I was able to speak with a nurse. She told me to give him fever medicine for the next 48 hours and if the fever didn't break after the weekend, make an appointment. I obeyed the doctor and gave him the fever medicine. It helped, but he still had a fever and he also had chills, he was shaking, and he spit up a couple of times. I continued to profess the blood of Jesus over my son and I knew that the devil couldn't cross the bloodline when you call on Jesus. You must know what to do when you can't get to a doctor's office because anything could happen. You also must teach them as they grow because they won't always be with you. You have to prepare them for life challenges when it comes to their health.

When we were growing up, my parents told my sibling and me to always recite **Isaiah 53:5b** *"and with his stripes we are healed." It does not matter what you see, it doesn't matter how you feel, by the stripes of Jesus, you are healed. I knew God loved me and sent his son Jesus to die for me for any sickness, disease, or pain.*

It didn't matter what the doctors said. We heard it but didn't receive negative news. Was it hard sometimes? Yes! When you're in pain or have discomfort, yes, but I still would say I am healed, whole, delivered and covered by the blood of Jesus. I am in my 30's and I still say this today!

Childrens' Prayer:

Father God, I know that Jesus died on the cross for all sickness, disease, and pain that might come my way. I know by the stripes of Jesus, I am healed. I welcome your healing anointing in my body right now. Every part of my body is strong in the Lord. I have divine health. I am covered by the blood of Jesus. I am healed from the crown of my head to the soles of my feet because Jesus died for me. Amen

Parents' Prayer:

Father, in the name of Jesus, I thank you for loving me so much and for sending your son Jesus to die for us. Jesus, who is a healer, who is our deliverer, and whose blood was shed on the cross for me and my children. I speak to my children's body right now and thank you that your angels are covering them from the crown of their heads to the soles of their feet. We have the blood that was shed for every sickness, disease *or pain that may try to attack my children's body. As believers, my children are sealed and protected by the blood of Jesus. In **Ps.107:20** – you sent your word and healed me and delivered me and my children from any destruction. I thank you Lord that my children are prospering and in good health, even as their soul prospers. In the name of Jesus, I curse every sickness, disease, germ, and virus that touches my body or my children's body. It will die instantly in Jesus' name, Amen.*

<u>Chapter 8 – Children Adjusting to Divorce</u>

In this life, children go through many things that is beyond their control, due to breakups within marriages and families. Those things include selfishness, arrogance, excessive pride from a parent, greed, and others disregarding the feelings of who's affected greatly by them. God is in the restoring business. He can restore happiness in you and your children's life and they can adjust well to the change. With God, all things are possible, and children can adjust with the right positive attitude in any negative situation with guidance from their parents. God doesn't choose for anyone! You have a choice in life to do what's right for you and your family or what's wrong by making decisions based on selfish reasons.

According to Healthychildren.org, when talking to your child about the divorce, follow these guidelines:

- *Be completely honest and open about what is happening. Talk about the divorce in simple terms.*
- *Make sure your child knows the divorce is not his/her fault.*
- *Try not to blame your ex-spouse or show anger.*
- *Be patient with their questions.*

You must continue to be honest with your children, letting them know that they are loved and not abandoned makes all the difference in the world. No one is perfect in this world and God knows that as well, but he does give us the free will to choose whether we will make good decisions or poor decisions. When children are going through these types of crises in their life, we must reassure them and commit to them that God loves and will carry them through that situation. He will give them peace in the mist of the storm.

Often, children have all types of emotions when things drastically change in their life, so you must teach them how to deal with their emotions. When they are feeling sad, angry, alone, unloved, or unwanted, you must teach them how to navigate those feelings. If you ask for God's help in a big situation like a divorce or starting over in a blended family, He will meet the need. God cares about our feelings and every part of our life's issues or problems.

I was married for 13 years and out of my marriage, I have two beautiful children whom I love dearly. One day, something happened, and I realized that soon my marriage would be over. I was not happy about it, but with God he brought me and my children through it. The number one thing that kept me focused was having a relationship with God, having my prayer time with God. It was important for me to have devotional time with my children every day, and teaching them that God loves them very much and mommy and daddy do as well. Due to me staying busy in church, attending on Sundays with the children, and having a consistent routine, the children and I were able to walk through that storm closer and better than ever.

At times, my children would become emotional and cry or feel like they were not enough. I told them that we would talk and express our feelings in words, but not in anger or resentment. Children go through things and feel many emotions and stress just like us as parents!

Going through my divorce, I constantly told my children that it was ok. That daddy made a choice that he thought was best for him, but God have us in his hands. So, when my children would feel sad or felt some type of way, we would sing happy songs about Jesus. We still do! Now, we sit around the table and play this game about using your words and how you feel with your highs and lows for the day. All I can say is I stay focused and expressed my feelings in a positive way with my children. I gave them extra love and care when needed to show them when big life challenges come at them, stay calm, think things through, pray about it, and then act.

<u>Childrens' Affirmation:</u> *I am accepted. I am enough. I am loved, because God loves me, and my parents do too. I accept this change as something good, not bad. I love my life, I love myself. I have a happy emotional state and I am adjusting well to different changes in my life. It will make me stronger. God's love for me has cast out all fear and doubt. He restores, in my life trust, hope and happiness with my mom, dad, and others. I am honest and free to speak how I feel, in love, with my mom, dad, and others. I pray that we come closer to each* *other to serve God's plan and purpose for me. Amen*

Parents' Prayer:

Father, in Jesus' name, I thank you that this new change in my life and family will be for your glory. Show me how to minister to my children to let them know that they are loved. I thank you that my children will grow and adapt quickly to this change. It will not affect their minds or bodies in any negative way. Show me how to meet my children's needs emotionally, physically, spiritually, and mentally through this process. Give me strength to show love at all times, not anger, resentment or pain. Let me not be afraid due to this change. I speak clarity and confidence into my children' lives, so they will know how to handle drastic change. Amen.

Chapter 9 – Children Adjusting to a Blended Family

Many breakups within marriages and families are due to selfishness, arrogance, excessive pride, and greed in society, which has children going through many unhealthy situations where they have to adjust the best way they can emotionally and physically. Children can adjust in a positive way without feeling abandonment but loved. There are many ways God can restore families even through a blended family.

According to Help Guide's article about bonding with your new blended family, children want to feel:

1. Safe and secure – Children want to be able to count on parents and stepparents. Children of divorce parents have already felt upset by people they trust for letting them down.

2. _Loved_- *Children like to see and feel your affection, although it should come in a gradual process.*

3. _Valued_- *Children often feel unimportant or invisible when it comes to decision-making in the new blended family. Recognize their role in the family when you make decisions.*

4. _Heard and emotionally connected_. – *Creating an honest and open environment, free of judgment, will help children feel heard and emotionally connected to a new stepparent. Show them that you can view the situation from their perspective.*

The new parents must reassure them of their strong commitment to the family. By building a relationship, in wholeness, by being honest, and always communicating will build trust and help them maintain a positive atmosphere. By having a heart to serve, regardless of getting something in return, new parents will show selflessness.

It is important, not to show favoritism, but treat all the children the same. Giving attention and reinforcing it with actions and positive words are a great way to build relationships.

Childrens' Affirmation:

I am accepted and loved by my new parents. I am glad God blessed me with this new family. I have a happy emotional state. I am adjusting well with my new family structure. God's love for me restores my life towards my new sisters, brothers and my new mom or dad. I love, trust and will be honest about how I feel through positive words. I pray that we come closer to each other to serve God's plan and purpose for my life. Amen

Parents' Prayer:

Father, in Jesus' name, I thank you that my new family grows stronger in love, trust, joy and commitment. Our children are loved emotionally, physically, spiritually, and mentally. Show our children how to be open and honest by communicating with each other in love and accepting change. Show my husband/wife how to be a good communicator and express themselves. My husband is a good initiator. I speak clarity and confidence into his life and spirit, so he can lead our family. I acknowledge you, God, to show us wisdom on how to work hard and show us how to be open to bringing all our children together as one family, for your glory. Amen

Chapter 10- God's Favor for your Life

All my life, I have been shown and taught to believe in God's favor. As a child, I had many situations where I had to be positive, regardless of the situation. **Proverbs 3:4** *says, so shall I find favor and good understanding and insight of God and man. I learned to profess favor with my teachers, students, and friends. In my 20's I was able to purchase a home with my sibling with no money down. We had favor. God's favor is much better than money. God sent certain people in my life to help me get it done. I had to trust God's word and stay on my profession daily. God, you said I don't need money, I need favor, and I believed it no matter what came my way.*

For example, just like you have a physical father that provides for you and meet your needs, we have a heavenly father that is there with us to supply all our needs and give us favor in life. All we have to do is trust God and believe in him and he will always work things out. He has done it for me countless times and have never failed me. **_Philippians 4:19_** *– But my God shall supply all your need according to his riches in glory by Christ Jesus. I brought that tradition to my children to do the same and to profess favor. God likes it when we talk to him because he wants to hear what is important to us. He is always listening, and He always hears. God loves us, He answers our prayers in the way that is best for us. Not our will, but His will for our life. We just have to be patient and trust him that his timing is best for us.*

You must remember, when you are believing for God's favor, you must watch your words over your kids and circumstance. If you are talking negative words you will not be able to live a prosperous life and have favor upon your life. When you have a negative thought about your kids or anything keep your mouth closed. Negative words can keep you and your children from the destiny that God has for you and your family.

In life, there is always two voices fighting for your attention. It is the voice of faith (positive words) or the voice of fear and defeat (negative words). During tough times, believe for God's favor on your life and children, be on guard with your mouth by choosing your words carefully. Through using positive words and trusting in God's word, his favor is limitless. That means, when you confess God's favor on your life and children, there's no limit to what God will do!

Everyday my children profess daily (before they go to school) that they are blessed and highly favored in the Lord. They profess that they will have favor with their teachers, classmates, and everybody they meet. No obstacle can stop them and they have supernatural increase in every area of their lives.

*Stand on **Psalms 5:12**. It says, "For you bless the righteous, O Lord; you cover him with favor as with a shield."*

Childrens' Prayer

Father, I thank you that today I choose victory! The voice of faith with positive words. You like it when I talk to you and trust in what you say. I can have what I say through my words that are positive that gives me power. I am blessed and highly favored in the Lord. I have favor with my teachers and classmates. When I feel someone doesn't like me or I am being treated unfairly, you crown me with favor each and every day. I know you hear me and love me every time I pray. In Jesus' name, Amen.

Childrens' Daily Affirmation

I CAN DO ALL THINGS THROUGH CHRIST WHO STRENGTHENS ME! NO WEAPON FORMED AGAINST ME SHALL PROSPER! I AM SMART. I CAN LEARN. I AM 10 TIMES BETTER THAN THE WORLD. I HAVE 20/20 VISION, PERFECT RECALL AND PERFECT HEARING.

I FIND FAVOR WITH MY TEACHERS AND CLASSMATES. I AM TAUGHT OF THE LORD. THE PEACE OF GOD IS UPON ME IN EVERY SENSE OF THE WORD – WHOLENESS, COMPLETENESS, NOTHING LACKING, NOTHING LOST IN ME. THE PEACE OF GOD GUIDES ME!

I LOVE MYSELF. I LOVE MY LIFE. I AM NOT LAZY. I AM AMAZING. I AM STRONG. I AM BEAUTIFUL. I AM HANDSOME. I AM A LEADER. I AM DISCIPLINED. I AM FOCUS. I AM A GOOD LISTENER. I FOLLOW DIRECTIONS THE FIRST TIME, EVEN WHEN IT'S HARD. I STICK WITH THINGS AND REFUSE TO QUIT.

I AM PROTECTED PHYSICALLY, SPIRITUALLY, MENTALLY, AND EMOTIONALLY. I AM COVERED BY THE BLOOD OF JESUS! I WILL KEEP MY HANDS,

FEET AND OTHER OBJECTS TO MYSELF. I WILL DO MY BEST TO HAVE A GREAT DAY.

ABOUT ALISON

Alison Womack is the author of Winning in Life: Helping your children to put God first when dealing with life's challenges and also, I am a Super Hero Strong: Everyday of the Week! She is the proud mother of two and loves motivating children. Alison enjoys spending time with her family and working in ministry and is an entrepreneur. She enjoys designing wardrobes, homes, and coordinating events.

Made in the USA
Columbia, SC
29 March 2023